"Although everyone expresses the importance of family engagement, not everyone knows how to achieve it. Muhs offers a comprehensive practical how-to guide that is sure to offer insights to both novice and veteran early childhood educators."

> —Valora Washington, PhD, CAE, chief executive officer,
> Council for Professional Recognition

"Family engagement is a critical part of any child care business. Both new and experienced family child care providers will find Muhs's concise guide useful in their efforts to build stronger relationships with parents."

> —Bill Hudson, chief executive officer, National Association
> for Family Child Care

"Family engagement is vital for the successful education of children. Mary has clearly captured the important elements of building and maintaining wonderful relationships with families. This book is a useful and practical resource—a must for trainers, mentors, coaches, and college educators. It is absolutely a high-priority read for family child care providers and center staff."

> —Eva Daniels, family child care consultant, community college
> adjunct faculty, former executive director of the National
> Association for Family Child Care

"Mary Muhs gives well-researched and relevant insight about how to engage families in all types of situations, as well as teaching educators how to create opportunities out of challenges. Strengthening family communication and engagement is an important aspect of early childhood care and education, and I recommend those involved in the field to read this book."

> —Carla Rogg, president, ProSolutions Training, the professional
> development division of Care Solutions, Inc.

"This book is a great educational tool for those of us in the field. Mary reveals different angles to view family engagement and steps for overcoming barriers. You will appreciate her depth of knowledge and generosity in sharing effective methods for building healthy family engagement."

> —Linda Bartos King, executive director, Love to Grow On

Family Engagement in Early Childhood Settings

Redleaf *Quick* Guide

Family Engagement in Early Childhood Settings

Mary Muhs

Redleaf Press®
www.redleafpress.org
800-423-8309

Published by Redleaf Press
10 Yorkton Court
St. Paul, MN 55117
www.redleafpress.org

First edition 2019
Cover design by Jim Handrigan
Cover photo by iStock/MStudioImages
Typeset in Signo and Avenir by Douglas Schmitz
Printed in the United States of America

Library of Congress Cataloging-in-Publication Data

Names: Muhs, Mary, author.
Title: Family engagement in early childhood settings / Mary Muhs.
Description: First edition. | St. Paul, MN : Redleaf Press, 2018. | Includes
   bibliographical references.
Identifiers: LCCN 2018026355 (print) | LCCN 2018044900 (ebook) | ISBN
   9781605546063 (electronic) | ISBN 9781605546056 (pbk.)
Subjects: LCSH: Early childhood education—Parent participation. |
   Parent-teacher relationships. | Home and school. | Motivation in education.
Classification: LCC LB1139.35.P37 (ebook) | LCC LB1139.35.P37 M843 2018
   (print) | DDC 372.21—dc23

Printed on acid-free paper   U24-01

I dedicate this work to my parents, my family, my husband, Tom, and my daughter, Naomi, from whom I have learned the importance of trust, values, culture, and, most of all, love.

CONTENTS

INTRODUCTION: A CULTURE OF FAMILY ENGAGEMENT

"It takes a village to raise a child."

—African proverb

Working with parents and families can be a challenge, especially when contradicting expectations or communication challenges exist. However, working together can also be a joyful and empowering experience for both the program and the family if partnering with families is built into the program's culture.

Building a culture of family engagement begins with the first contact a family has with a program and never ends. If family is woven into the fabric or culture of a program, the program will be as strong as it can possibly be.

What Is the Culture of a Program?

The term *culture* can be understood in several ways. Among these are the following definitions (*Merriam-Webster* 2017):

> "The integrated pattern of human knowledge, belief, and behavior that depends upon the capacity for learning and transmitting knowledge to succeeding generations."

> "The customary beliefs, social forms, and material traits of a racial, religious, or social group."

> "The characteristic features of everyday existence (such as diversions or a way of life) shared by people in a place or time."

> "The set of shared attitudes, values, goals, and practices that characterizes an institution or organization."

In an early childhood education and care program, culture is the interconnectedness among all the pieces and parts of the program: families, educators, children, environment, policies, curriculum, outdoor spaces, food, and more. The program's culture is how all the pieces work together, interact, and exist. As the last definition in the list above states, culture goes even deeper as well. It is a shared understanding of values and goals—or, in the case of early childhood education programs, a shared understanding of how children learn and grow and what constitutes education for young children. Families and educators should find the program's philosophy and mission a match to their own, consisting of principles they can support and promote. Additionally culture is present in the shared attitudes and values of all the participants. Families who value academic pursuits may not be the right fit for a program that values artistic pursuits more strongly. Likewise a program that promotes high family engagement may not suit families who live far away and are not able to actively engage in program events.

The culture of a program can be seen and felt from the first encounter. When the culture of a program is positive and strong, it permeates the community with a palpable energy. A program with a strong culture will have a well-known and developmentally appropriate philosophy that people can see in action as soon as they enter the program. The community sees the program as a model for high-quality programming and a place to enroll children where they will be successful. In this way, the culture of a program can act as an indirect marketing tool. When the culture of a program is weak, the community sees it as a babysitter instead of an early childhood education program. A program with a weak culture does not employ consistent philosophy or policies, has high educator turnover, and struggles to maintain full enrollment. A program with a weak culture indirectly markets itself negatively to families seeking child care and education for their children.

Families are a key component of a program's culture. When families are integrated into the program's philosophy and mission along with children and educators, they help support the program. If families are not integrated into the program's culture, the program may feel off balance, operating without a key piece of support.

It is easy to assume that all programs honor families or incorporate them into the program philosophy and mission. Of course a family comes along with every child! However, there's a difference between having policies and procedures that merely include families and actually weaving families into the program's culture.

Every program must have traditional policies and procedures for family engagement. These may include everything from requirements for families to provide children's health documentation to how families can contact their children's teacher. Some programs may require family members to participate in or donate their time to the program as part of the enrollment agreement, while others may offer only traditional family participation events, such as an annual parent-teacher conference. While these policies and procedures are necessary to support the overall program structure, much more can be done to bring the entire family into the fold.

Strengthening the Culture of Family Engagement

According to early childhood researchers Douglas Powell and Patrick O'Leary (2009), the following structural principles together can create a strong cultural fabric of family engagement, helping the program succeed:

- Programs must serve the entire family.

- A program must know and accommodate the overall community demographics.

- The hallmark of healthy family engagement is trust between the educator and the families.

- Educators must see children and their families as unique.

- Parents are not just parents, but people.

- Families perceive engagement differently than programs do.

- The quality of a program is in the eye of the beholder.

- Educators need support and professional development around family engagement and communication.

Programs Must Serve the Entire Family

Children do not enroll on their own, nor do they exist connected only to their parents. Instead they come with extended families, traditions, experiences, histories, values, and beliefs. How do your policies and procedures meet children's family expectations or experiences? How do they conflict? While you may not know everything about children's families, especially at the start, your efforts at cultivating a relationship with each child must include the child's entire family.

A Program Must Know and Accommodate the Overall Community Demographics

Whether your program is part of a larger corporation or is a stand-alone family child care, it must reflect the needs of the community it serves. This is a wise business strategy and an educational best practice. No program can serve every family perfectly. Not all families will be perfect for your program, and your program may not be perfect for every family. Just as early childhood educators make sure their programs are developmentally appropriate for children, they must also make sure they are appropriate for the children's families. How can your program better accommodate the community demographics?

The Hallmark of Healthy Family Engagement Is Trust between the Educator and the Families

Families must be able to trust the educators who care for their children. Educators must also trust that families are doing the best they can by their children. Judgments about parenting capability can cloud trust. It is important to work on building trust by communicating openly, asking questions, encouraging sharing of stories, and providing supportive information and help. How can your program open up opportunities to build trust?

Educators Must See Children and Their Families as Unique

Just as no two children are alike, no two families are alike. Creating opportunities for under-standing and knowing each family as a separate entity builds trust between families and educators. When you're getting to know a family, it is helpful to learn about their personal expectations and hopes for their child. What are their goals? Goals may be similar from family to family, but the reasons behind the goals may differ—and these reasons are important to know. What are families' reasons, and how can you build their goals into your program? Does your program offer opportunities to meet one-on-one with families throughout their time in the program? Do these one-on-one meetings provide a chance to share stories and experiences so both educators and family members get to know the whole child?

Parents Are Not Just Parents, but People

One of the most overlooked aspects of building a culture of family engagement is the chance to give back to the parents. Parents are, of course, participating in your program because of their child, but at the same time, they are also parents, adults, and individuals. They have names other than Ms. or Mr., Mom or Dad. Providing for their needs and interests can promote a culture of curiosity, problem solving, and community. How can your program build up parents by offering what they need to become better parents or better adults so they can, in turn, offer better versions of themselves to their children?

Families Perceive Engagement Differently Than Programs Do

Program staff tend to perceive family engagement in terms of what the family can do for the program, while families see family engagement in terms of what the program can do to get them involved. Programs must consider time, access, money, and perceived ability in making decisions about expected family engagement. It is important to provide a variety of opportunities by a variety of means. Find ways to be flexible and accommodating of all needs. For example, when asking families to attend an event, has your program considered child care for other children, transportation costs, families' regular routines, work schedules, physical access, and needs of other family members?

The Quality of a Program Is in the Eye of the Beholder

When programs seek to improve their quality, often they look to professional tools, standards, and assessments for guidance. Usually those tools and standards will include considerations for how programs can improve relationships and family engagement. However, not all tools and standards consider what families need or what families believe needs to be improved. Family perspectives are often reduced to a simple survey—or nothing at all. Including parents and other family members in program improvement provides a well-rounded perspective and helps ensure that families remain woven into the program culture. How does your program include families in the quality improvement process? How can you include family perspectives in a more consistent manner?

Educators Need Support and Professional Development around Family Engagement and Communication

Educators are well trained and educated in curriculum, child development, child interactions, and guiding behaviors, but how well are teachers educated on effective communication and interaction with parents and other family members? Early childhood education and care is ultimately a service field. It is built on relationships with children, families, and colleagues. The educator role is also an emotional one, with strong ties to children and their families. When a program provides educators ongoing support and education around communication, relationship building with families, family structure, diversity, and problem solving, the program's culture of family engagement grows stronger.

A Note on Language

Children live in many kinds of families. They may live with one or two parents. They may live with a stepparent, guardian, or adult relative. This book sometimes uses the word *parents.* When you see this word, think of the adult(s) children live with who take care of them.

No Two Families Are Alike

It makes sense to remind ourselves regularly that no two families are alike. Each family is made up of unique individuals who are working together to raise a child. When we are building a culture of family engagement, we need to look at each family as unique and special, offering its own culture to the world. Each of the following family types may be a part of your program's culture, and no one type of family is more or less important than another. Here are just a few of the many possible types of families in your program:

- families with one child

- families with multiple children

- blended families

- families with adopted children

- LGBTQ families

- two-parent families

- single-parent families

- families with children raised by nonparent relatives

- multigenerational families

- foster families

- English-speaking families

- non-English-speaking families

- multilingual families

- families with children with special needs

- families who are refugees

- families with first-time parents

- families with experienced parents

Where Does a Program Begin When Developing a Culture of Family Engagement?

Begin with research and literature as a foundation. The National Association for the Education of Young Children (NAEYC) provides guidance in how programs should work closely with families to be responsive, share developmental information, make decisions, and be involved in their children's experiences and education. NAEYC also reminds programs to use developmentally appropriate practice (DAP) in all aspects of caring for children. DAP includes practices that are age appropriate, individually appropriate, and culturally appropriate (Copple and Bredekamp 2009).

The NAEYC Code of Ethical Conduct reminds educators of the importance of truly knowing a family and their expectations for their child (NAEYC 2011). Programs and families do not have to be perfectly happy with or agree on everything, but each side should extend respect and trust that the other side is putting the best interests of the children first.

We must remember that children do not come to programs all alone but with families supporting their efforts. Research tells us that a child's development can be enriched when educators and parents agree on how the child should be cared for and educated (Copple and Bredekamp 2009; Heick 2013). Both sides should make every effort to come to an understanding on behalf of the child.

Choose a Strength-Based Approach to Build a Culture of Family Engagement

It is often easier to look at families from the areas of weakness or challenges they face than to view families from the point of view of their strengths. A strength-based approach to working with families focuses the educator on family strengths—what they already have in place, what they do well, and how they are already successful. Even the families most challenged in life have abundant strength somewhere. Shifting your focus to supporting and enhancing family strengths can also help improve their areas of weakness.

A strength-based approach is a conscious shift in perspective. It may look something like this:

Challenge-Based Approach	Strength-Based Approach
A child lives with an extended family of eight in a two-bedroom apartment.	The child knows and develops a relationship with grandparents and great-grandparents.
A child's mother works two jobs to pay rent and put food on the table.	The child's mother has two jobs and is able to provide for her family.

In the latter example, by focusing on the fact that the child's mother is working two jobs as something positive, we can validate her efforts to build a strong family. Considering that we hope she can spend more time with her child and that her employment may not be able to change, we can ask ourselves the following questions: What can we, as educators, say and do to support her ongoing efforts? How can we find small ways to help her engage with her child more?

It Takes a Village

In the family systems theory, which is a combination of developmental and ecological perspectives, families do not exist alone but in conjunction with and influenced by the systems surrounding them (Walsh 2004). Just as children are surrounded and supported by their parents, siblings, and other family members, families themselves are surrounded and supported by their neighborhood, community, and so on. In early childhood education, family systems theory may look something like the following illustration:

A Family Systems Theory for Children in Early Childhood Education Programs

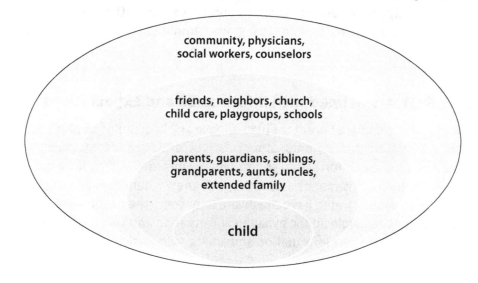

community, physicians,
social workers, counselors

friends, neighbors, church,
child care, playgroups, schools

parents, guardians, siblings,
grandparents, aunts, uncles,
extended family

child

For educators, realizing where families exist in relation to their children is important. Parents are a child's first teachers and primary caregivers. Early childhood education exists to support, enhance, and lift up families—which, in turn, will support a child's positive growth and development.

Overcoming Barriers to Building a Culture of Family Engagement

No matter how well we plan for family engagement, there will be barriers or challenges that may prohibit or restrict family engagement opportunities. These barriers are considerable, but they may not be permanent. Looking at these barriers to family engagement as challenges that can be overcome will set the right attitude for helping families be stronger than ever.

Parents Have Varied Knowledge Bases on Parenting and Child Development

Parents often say that they know about parenting from how they were raised by their parents. Naturally parents rely on what they remember from childhood or what they hear from their parents as adults. However, parents are not all equal, and their remembered or shared experiences may not match what is now known to be best practice. With time comes research and new evidence on child development, guidance and discipline, social and emotional development, and learning. What was best practice in the past may not be best practice now. Parents may not know what they do not know until they need to know it, so helping parents marry their upbringing with current research is the key. Providing current research in newsletters, at conferences, and in documentation will help parents connect the old and the new.

Families May Not Have the Resources to Make Different or Better Choices

Not all family situations are the same. Economic circumstances influence the ability parents have to seek support and resources for their family. Transportation limits access to services or materials. When resources are restricted, families are not able to act on their desires or even their needs. Family participation in events, conferences, and other daily engagement may not be possible. Find ways for families to engage without cost, with less time, and from wherever they are.

Parents May Be Overwhelmed with Information and Expectations

Parents do not have to complete parent training or have any knowledge of parenting before starting a family. They have their parents, other relatives, and friends for support and advice. They also have a multitude of information sources on the Internet. All the information at hand can be overwhelming, and many parents may not know whom they can trust. Parenting expectations are high. Most parents have the desire to become the best parents they can be, but it can be a challenge to juggle all the available information and know what to do. Help parents navigate toward the best information and advice, and work together to help them be the best parents possible.

CHAPTER 1: MAKING A FIRST IMPRESSION

Pasqual is two years old. He and his family are visiting the early childhood program for the first time. His father carries him into the center. His mother pushes his little sister, who is six months old, in a stroller. Pasqual's grandmother walks a couple of steps behind, taking it all in. Pasqual holds his favorite blanket tightly in his arms. He is quiet as he takes it all in. Up until now, Pasqual's grandmother was his primary caregiver. Since she will have to return to her home country soon, Pasqual's parents are visiting early childhood programs in search of full-time child care for both children.

To young children, their family is their world, their first teacher. In order to best serve the children, programs must serve the families first. A family comes as a package—it may be large or small, whole or broken.

First Impressions

A first impression can make or break a relationship. An old saying tells us it takes only seven seconds to make that first impression last. Only seven seconds! That is hardly enough time to blink, let alone to really make a good first impression on another person. But those seven seconds are important because making a good first impression with families can have a long-lasting effect on a child. First impressions start even before a family makes their first in-person visit.

Websites

Early childhood programs should have active and interactive websites for families to connect with before, during, and after their enrollment. Websites and other electronic media can profoundly influence communication, engagement, community building, information sharing, and involvement in program activities, and they can even give parents the resources they need to be better parents (Donohue 2017). To be effective, websites must be welcoming! A website is often the first—and sometimes the only—contact parents have with the program. Websites must do the following:

- Provide basic information about the center hours and location, including a phone number and email address.

- Describe the philosophy and mission of the program.

- Reflect the culture and vision of the program.

- Describe the curriculum and developmental competencies by age.

- Include administrators' and educators' qualifications and biographies.

- Provide a calendar of events or activities.

- Offer parent and family testimonials.

- Post educational information on child development and parenting.

- Provide credible resources and links for additional information searches.

- Offer photos of the program's environment and activities. (Make sure any photos of children have legal clearance and parental permission for posting on the Internet for advertising purposes.)

Social Media

A social media presence is a helpful way to share your program with the community and your families. For new families, social media may offer only a brief glimpse or snapshot into your program. For enrolled families, social media can provide a valuable informal glimpse into your program's daily operations. It can also help connect your enrolled families with one another. No matter how you employ social media, be sure to consider the following safety and confidentiality rules:

- Use photos of children only with prior written consent from the children's parents or guardians, and only for the express purpose of social media. Consult an attorney for legal language and requirements for your state. Private social media accounts are a safe alternative. Only those who request and are granted permission (such as enrolled families) may follow a private social media account.

- Never share children's real names or identifying information.

- Post about an event after the event has occurred rather than during the event to avoid identifying in real time locations where children are gathering.

- If you're using social media for advertising, consider two social media accounts: a public one for prospective families and a private one for enrolled families. The account for prospective families can be more general and can provide a connection to the program website for additional information. The account for enrolled families can offer glimpses into their children's day using photos and more specific information.

Email

Email communication has become the norm for families who have questions or who want to request further information to help them make a decision about enrollment. Emails enable fast written replies, limiting confusion and improving communication. Be sure to provide a positive and welcoming feel in your writing. Have you ever heard the old saying that you should be smiling through the phone when you answer it? The same goes for email. When you write, be sure that your intended tone is coming through clearly. Additionally you should respond to emails within twenty-four hours of receipt. Families are looking for the information they need to make their decisions on child care, so a timely response is important.

Phone Calls

Families are more likely to make first contact by phone than by stopping in for a surprise visit. This reality can be a challenge for programs, which must juggle the competing needs of answering the phone, conversing with families on the phone, and tending to the children in their care. A busy day may not allow for someone to be available by phone at all times, so it is critical that programs establish phone protocols for when program administrators are away or when time on the phone is not going to be possible. Here are some suggestions for establishing a positive phone protocol:

Center-Based Programs

- Designate an individual who will be responsible for answering the phone if the administrator is away.

- Create a phone response script with possible questions and answers.

- Conduct phone training so everyone who may possibly answer the phone answers with the appropriate greeting and knows how to support calls.

- Use a voice mail system and respond to voice mails within twenty-four hours of receipt.

Family Child Care Programs

- Use a voice mail system and respond to voice mails within twenty-four hours of receipt. Your outgoing message should mention that although you are with the children, you value every call, and you will return calls when you are able—always within twenty-four hours.

- Inform new families that you will have a phone available for emergencies and critical incoming calls but that you are not able to speak regularly during the day.

- Encourage texting for enrolled families to allow for brief messages but not conversations.

Open-Door Policy for All Families

No matter how families locate your program, welcoming families into your program can be a challenge. Naturally a new family will want and need to visit during regular business hours. Families will want to visit without prior notice to see what a regular day is like. An open-door policy honors this need and makes families feel welcome. Allowing families to visit on a whim can provide them with confidence and comfort that your program maintains the same level of quality at all times. Families can show up at the program's door for a tour or just a quick visit to gather information.

Center-Based Programs

An open-door policy for a center-based program is not challenging to establish, but it may seem overwhelming on busy days. When a family shows up at the door, staff may suddenly get nervous and may scramble to find an available teacher or director to help the family. How the program makes this happen smoothly, without visible stress, can make or break the family's first impression of the program. Set a protocol for what will happen if a family walks in to visit your program.

Who greets the family? What if the director is unavailable?

- Designate a staff member who will greet the family.

- Decide who should be the primary person to handle the family's visit.

- Determine in advance who will be available when the primary person is absent or unavailable.

- Make sure the family signs in to help you gather important follow-up information, such as contact information, ages of children, and special questions.

What will you provide for the visiting family?

- Prepare packets of information in advance and have them always at the ready.

- Include packets for each age group or program, such as pre-K or after school.

How will you give a tour if no staff member is available to be away from the children?

- Decide in advance how to welcome a family and give a tour if no one is available. For example, perhaps the tour will need to take place in a single classroom.

- Remember, the first impression is the key to starting a strong program-family relationship, so use your best customer service skills. Smile and introduce yourself and the program. Ask your visitors questions, such as their names, their children's ages, where they live, and how they found your program. If children are present, engage them with a smile and personal introduction. Thank the family for visiting and let them know you will follow up with more information, answers to their questions, and another chance to tour the program if you were unable to accommodate that request.

- Provide follow-up after the family leaves the program. Within twenty-four hours of the impromptu visit, send the family an email. Thank them for visiting. Answer their questions. Provide additional helpful information or invite them to return for another visit. Let them know you hope to talk with them again, or confirm the next contact or visit.

Family Child Care Programs

Determine your open-door policy in advance. This is a bit trickier in family child care programs than in center-based programs, since a family child care provider is often alone or working with only one additional adult. An open-door policy with a family child care program may simply be an opportunity to stop by the home during business hours to make a quick visit or observe. Family child care providers will need to be prepared to welcome and greet families who stop by unannounced, even though they may not be able to provide a complete tour or answer all questions. Preparation should include the following:

- Know in advance what you want to say if a family stops in during business hours.

- Assemble in advance packets of information about your family child care, including your biography, program philosophy, policies, and tuition rates. Have the packets ready to offer to anyone who stops by.

- Have a means for families to sign in and provide needed information for follow-up. Gather names, contact details, and children's ages.

- Follow up by phone or email within twenty-four hours to set up an additional meeting to answer questions and go over your program philosophy and specifics.

CHAPTER 2: LEARNING ABOUT ONE ANOTHER

Solveig is a four-year-old child who is attending a full-day preschool for the first time. She has previously been home with one parent while the other parent has been working outside the home. Now both parents are working full time. Solveig is excited to start preschool and meet new friends. She is also a little worried that the other children might not like her, since her family is different from many families. Solveig has two dads. She feels lucky to have such loving parents. Perhaps her parents will get to come to her preschool sometime and meet the other parents. She hopes the preschool has a big sandbox and a mud kitchen. Solveig loves to make mud pies and sell them to her friends to raise money for the community shelter.

In the scenario above, how could you learn more about Solveig's family? What would you want to know? Why would it be important to learn about Solveig and her family?

Once families have enrolled in your program, it is time to learn about one another and continue to build relationships. Building relationships with the families in your program never ends, because the children, family members, and program grow and change naturally over time. Establishing multiple touch points for families from the first day to the last will support changing needs and expectations, ensure that your program responds to every family, and help every family stay engaged.

Intake Meetings and Experiences

One of the most critical components of family engagement is immediately establishing a give-and-take rapport through an initial meeting of parents and educators. This intake meeting can vary in format, but it should happen before the child's first day rather than on the first day. Time set aside for a private meeting between the parents and the child's main caregiver in your program is preferred. Think of this time as a chance for both parties to learn about one another. Both should feel comfortable asking questions and sharing information. Ask open-ended questions when possible, as this meeting should be a conversation rather than an interrogation.

Learn about the family's and child's strengths by asking questions about the following aspects of their family life:

- family members living at home

- parental working arrangements

- home community

- child's interests and talents

- family daily schedules

Discover family cultural preferences and expectations by asking about these subjects:

- routines and traditions

- religious preferences

- communication preferences

Discover the child's personality in the parents' eyes with questions about the following:

- child's interests and talents

- child's fears

- developmental history

- child's daily schedule and routine

- hopes and dreams the parents have for their child

Discover the parents' expectations and preferences regarding these topics:

- daily care, including feeding, eating, toileting, and cleanliness

- education

- peers and social situations

- communication

Share your program philosophy and goals with the family, connecting these to the family's philosophy and goals as much as possible. Share your program policies on the following issues:

- communication

- illnesses and absences

- tuition and finances

- age-specific issues, such as infant feeding, toddler biting, and preschool toilet learning

- licensing and accreditation (where appropriate)

Take notes at this meeting and share them with all educators caring for the child. Make it clear that the information is confidential and not to be shared outside the program or with other families in the program. Intake meeting notes are the key to establishing a positive long-term relationship with a family—a relationship in which the parents feel connected to the program and the educators care about the whole child's well-being. Refer to these notes as you encounter changes that might affect this relationship, such as changes in the child's development, family challenges, and transitions to the next age group within the program. Consider how these changes may affect the child or the family based on the family's expectations, desires for their child, or religious and cultural preferences. Revisit certain questions during conferences or arranged meetings to keep current and ensure that the relationship stays strong.

Establishing Expectations

It's important to remember that both the program and the family have expectations. Although the family chooses to enroll in the program, the program must consider the family expectations to ensure there is a match, or "goodness of fit." Families often come to a program on the recommendation of friends or relatives, believing that the program will be perfect for them as well. This may not be the case. Taking time to explore expectations before a child begins a program will help parents determine whether the program is indeed a good fit for their child. When a family and child are the right fit for a program, they become a valuable source of marketing, are likely to be strong advocates, will be more engaged, and are more likely to volunteer in the program from day one (Kenny 2014). Taking the opportunity and the time to communicate expectations between families and the program is well worth the effort.

Feedback Loops

Establishing a strong family engagement program is not just about whether family members participate in events or donate time. It goes far deeper. A key part of family engagement is involving parents in the day-to-day happenings of the program. To do this, a program needs to actively solicit feedback and ideas and intentionally offer opportunities to bring families into the program.

Surveys

Surveys provide an opportunity to solicit anonymous feedback from families. Typically surveys ask multiple-choice or short-answer questions about specific issues, situations, and policies. They are meant to provide a chance to offer quick feedback that can be quantified easily. The benefits of surveys include timeliness, cost effectiveness, simplicity, and confidentiality. The drawbacks of surveys include simple answers with no chance for clarification and confidentiality with no option for direct follow-up.

Programs often conduct surveys at key times when they need feedback to assess processes or events, such as after enrollment begins, when enrollment ends, and before or after a transition. A survey can also be employed as a check for satisfaction in a program, such as with an accreditation self-study process. Surveys can be distributed on paper or online through web-based survey applications. Online surveys provide convenience for programs and families. Families receive a link to the survey by email. Survey apps offer automated calculation and data gathering, making it easier for programs to collect and analyze the findings.

Parent Groups

Some programs offer an opportunity for parents to gather and share experiences and feedback on important program issues. Establishing a parent group can be a leap of faith, since it may feel as though it is an invitation for concerns and complaints. On the contrary, parents who connect with other parents experiencing similar circumstances build community. In this community, they find strength to be better parents and tend to be happier with the program overall. Parent groups can discuss anything from supporting new families to bringing in outside enrichment programs. A parent group should be led by the program director or a staff member, and it should offer chances for targeted feedback each session. Parent group meetings need not occur frequently: three to four times per year is usually sufficient. Parent groups can meet more often during times of change or improvement, such as during an accreditation self-study. Parent groups must establish a set of confidentiality rules to prevent personal issues from becoming topics of group discussion. Directors will want to ensure that if parents have specific concerns about their child's situation, those concerns are discussed privately.

When you are establishing a parent group for your program, include parents of children from each age group in a child care center or a balanced representation of parents in a family child care. Remember that this is a chance for parents to get to know one another while supporting the program that is so important to their child.

Parent Education Opportunities

Early childhood education programs not only support child development, but they also support parent development. Providing a means for supporting parental skills is a valuable way to give back to the families in a program. Programs can also learn a great deal about families' needs and preferences from their responses to parent education opportunities.

Lunch and Learn

A lunch and learn is a common type of parent education event. For a center-based child care, it may mean offering parents a chance to bring a sack lunch and spend some time learning about guiding children's behavior or toilet learning. For a family child care, it may mean inviting parents to join the group for lunch and observing what is happening in the program or learning fingerplays or basic American Sign Language (ASL). For both types of program, the time for a lunch and learn is limited by parent lunch breaks and program schedules. Here are ten possible lunch and learn topics:

* toilet learning

- parenting multiple children

- guidance and discipline strategies

- picky eaters

- welcoming a second or third child

- reading and literacy at home

- what to do if you suspect your child has a special need

- math activities to do at home

- sensory activities for toddlers at home

- ASL basics

Curriculum Night

A curriculum night occurs after program hours. It provides parents with hands-on examples of their children's daily activities. Examples of activities are available for parents to try, along with descriptions of the learning benefits and standards associated with each activity. A curriculum night is also a time to share program goals, learning objectives, and other curriculum information with parents. Providing photos and children's work samples will also help connect families to the curriculum. When parents get involved in their children's learning journey, they become trusted advocates and believers in the program's effectiveness. Here are five curriculum night ideas:

- **Family planting night:** Parents and children help plant playground garden plots. Families may donate materials and seeds, or the program can use donations from a local greenhouse. Schedule additional nights for weeding and harvesting, with stories and songs about plants and nature. Share science and math competencies children are experiencing through this activity.

- **Autumn sensory night:** Parents and children gather to explore pumpkins, corn, and other autumn nature materials, experiencing learning opportunities in all the developmental domains: physical, intellectual, language, emotional, and social. Activities vary by age group and may include a sensory table with pumpkin parts; measuring pumpkins' circumference and weight; sorting corn; creating art with leaves, seeds, and corn; and much more.

- **Art exhibit:** This child-created art exhibit is a chance for parents to learn about the benefits of open-ended art experiences for children. Children create a variety of artworks using multiple media, such as paintings, collages, and sculptures. All ages take part in developmentally appropriate art experiences. Educators take photos of the creation process, documenting learning experiences in writing. Educators display the documentation along with the art. To add an additional service component, art may be sold via silent auction, with proceeds going to a local charity or to supplement funds for new playground equipment, for example.

- **Transition nights:** This opportunity is offered over several nights, with each night devoted to a different age group. Each age group invites the children in the next-younger age group to visit their program and meet the educators. This night allows parents and children to visit the next age group in preparation for their eventual transition. Each age group offers hands-on activities showcasing the goals and interests of children at that age. Information about the daily schedule, activities, and procedures is provided, especially around specific age-group needs, such as napping, feeding, toilet learning, and outside play. If possible parents can be present from the older age group to help welcome the transitioning families and answer questions. Transition nights can be offered several times per year to allow for transitions at different times.

- **Family fun and movie night:** A family fun and movie night brings parents and children together to watch a short movie featuring the children themselves engaged in their daily fun at the program. Prior to the movie night, educators create short movies featuring the children interacting and participating in daily activities at the program. Then they show the movies to parents and children during the event. Educators also serve age-appropriate snacks and provide other hands-on activities for parents and children to experience together. A family fun and movie night is a great chance to showcase the daily learning children experience and how they grow and interact with one another. Showcasing favorite activities to do together invites parents to learn more about their children's day.

Educational Webinars

An educational webinar is a means of involving parents in a program from a distance. When parents cannot physically be at a program due to work location, transportation, or personal commitments, it does not necessarily mean they do not want to be engaged in the program. Often they look for ways to be involved without having to be physically present. Educational webinars are a means by which programs can share important information with parents remotely. An Internet webinar service can help parents and teachers gather from remote locations to learn about strategies to address biting, basic ASL, or establishing morning routines. Webinars offer parents a chance to not only connect with one another, but also to learn supportive parenting information. These benefits help parents see your program as a valuable resource. The program becomes a beacon for child development and parental support versus merely a place they bring their children for child care. Here are ten possible webinar topics:

- an introduction to your program's curriculum approach

- a day in the life of an infant, toddler, preschooler, or school-age child

- biting

- ASL for babies and toddlers

- creating morning routines with your child

- activities to support early writing at home

- supporting children through a natural disaster or trauma

- developmental domains for different age groups

- what to do if you believe your child has a special need

- encouraging literacy development at home

CHAPTER 3: SHARING DAILY EVENTS AND OCCURRENCES

The Palermo family is planning to visit the family child care located in their neighborhood. A neighbor recommended the caregiver and knows that openings will be available soon. For the Palermos, having both their baby and their toddler in the same program and near their home and work is important. They are looking for a homelike environment for their children. When their baby was born prematurely, they were worried they would lose her. They never spent a day away from the hospital. Then they discovered their nanny was improperly disciplining their toddler while they were at the hospital. It has been a rough year, and they just want a program they can trust. They are hoping this new family child care will be the place.

When families enroll in a program, they trust that the program will take care of their children. They trust that the program will treat their children with the same love and care families provide. But families have no way to know what is actually happening with their children every day—unless the program lets them know. Without continual and responsive communication between families and the program, parents will lose trust. Communication is critical to creating and maintaining family engagement.

Confidentiality and Ethics

Confidentiality is extremely important to establishing trust and building relationships. Early childhood educators are in a unique position of knowing parents and children closely. They should never share information about a family with another family, uninvolved colleagues, or others outside the program.

Early childhood educators often face ethical issues in their work with young children and their families. They must carefully balance their personal values and morals with those of the families in their care. NAEYC's Code of Ethical Conduct gives educators a framework for making ethical decisions using common core values that support children, families, and colleagues. These values include seeing childhood as a special and valuable time of life, using research on child development as a base of practice, recognizing the importance of a child's family bond, and seeing children in the context of their family, community, and culture. Additionally educators must respect children's diversity and uniqueness while developing relationships based on respect and trust (NAEYC 2011). For an early childhood educator who values the family and the place of the child within that family, it is a critical responsibility to establish communication, collaboration, and cooperation between families and educators (NAEYC 2011). In turn this partnership will promote family engagement and support children's development.

Effective Daily Communication

Daily communication with families should be positive and honest. It should be brief yet informative. When you are sharing a description of a child's day with a parent, it is important to both report on the positive and comment constructively on challenges in a manner that respects the child and the parent. No matter how challenging a child's behavior may be, maintaining a positive outlook will help a great deal in supporting your partnership with the family. Before communicating any information to parents about their child's day, consider a few key questions. The answers to these questions may influence how and when you communicate the information:

- **Is the information about typical child development and behaviors?** Parents always want to know whether their children are developing in a typical way. Make sure to mention when the behavior is not alarming or concerning. Help ease parents' fears. When the information you are sharing is not about typical child development or behavior, carefully consider the right time, place, and message to deliver it.

- **Is the information about typical child development and behavior that is showing up more consistently today?** This question is important to consider when you are talking about behavior that is typical but that is showing up more intensely or frequently. Perhaps you are addressing a child's hitting. Hitting on its own is developmentally appropriate, although not desirable. When hitting becomes so frequent that it interrupts the child's day or becomes so intense that it leaves a bruise on another child, it becomes a more important issue. When addressing a sensitive topic like this, choose a private and calm time to share information.

- **Are other children involved in the information you plan to share with parents?** When other children are involved and the communication is constructive information, it is critical to look for a private time to talk, maintaining confidentiality and not sharing names. If you are sharing positive information and another child is involved, be sure to share the same information with parents of all children involved.

- **Do you have both positive and constructive information to share?** Whenever you are sharing constructive information or concerns with families, always share positive information, too. Help parents see that the challenge you are sharing is only a small part of their child's day.

- **What do you gain by sharing the information with parents?** Are you communicating important information? Is the concern ongoing or increasing in intensity, or is it just a one-time situation? Are you asking the parents for their help or support?

- **What can you do to support the child based on this information?** Whenever you are sharing constructive information with parents about their child's development or behavior, always provide details on what you and the program are doing to support the child's needs. Are you already reviewing the daily schedule to minimize waiting and transitions? Are you already tracking those particular times of day when the child needs the most guidance to look for patterns? If you are communicating only concerns or constructive information, you are just passing the problem off to parents—and they are not present during the day to help solve the problem. Instead describe what you have already been doing and communicate how you want to partner with parents to support their child's success.

- **Why are you sharing the information right now, today (assuming it doesn't involve injury to another child)?** Is it because you were more frustrated with behavior today, or is it because you are truly concerned for the child's well-being? Can you write down this information instead and track it for a few days to see if it is an ongoing concern before sharing it?

If you take the time to consider these questions before communicating any information to parents, you can avoid crying wolf and alarming parents too early or sharing constructive information without purpose. Next let's look at strategies for communicating needed information to parents.

Timing

The timing of information sharing can make or break the relationship between parents and program. On a daily basis, programs have three opportunities for sharing information: drop-off, naptime, and pickup. Each of these times of day offers benefits and drawbacks. Examining what happens at each time of day may help clarify which will work better for sharing different types of information. In addition educators may arrange a specific time and place to meet with a parent for information sharing.

Drop-Off

This time of day is the busiest for parents. They are often hurried from preparing their children for the day and transporting them to the program. Sometimes they are running late and may make only a brief appearance in the program. It is also a busy time for educators, as children are arriving and breakfast is being served.

Sharing very brief positive information at drop-off time is appropriate. Here's an example: "Good morning, Ms. Gundlach! Good morning, Charlie!" The teacher smiles and bends down to see the child eye to eye. "It's great to see you this morning. Ms. Gundlach, today we are excited to continue to work on writing in our journals." Save constructive information for later in the day or for a scheduled meeting time devoted to that family.

Naptime

In a center-based program, naptime can allow educators to make phone calls or send emails or texts to parents sharing information about the children's day. For family child care providers, naptimes can vary based upon the ages of the children in the group. In either case, educators can use downtime during the day to provide updates on a child's day and send daily care notes on feedings, diaper changes, toilet learning, or rest. When teachers send information via email or text, they should be careful not to alarm parents or to share only constructive information with no accompanying positive information. Emails and text messages can be misread easily, so educators should write them carefully.

Pickup

The end of a child's day is often the most relaxed, and parents will often have more time to talk then. Nevertheless this may not always be the best time to share information—especially constructive information. After a long day at work, parents are not always in a great place to hear about challenges their child is having. Depending upon the information being shared and answers to the questions listed on page 24, educators should decide what to say and when to say it based upon the best interest of the child. Positive information is always welcome and will always support relationship building and engagement. When teachers need to share constructive information at pickup time, taking parents aside will help provide confidentiality and enough time to share.

Here's one example: "Good afternoon, Mr. Ramirez. How was your day today? Today was a busy day for Angel. She was active with her friends in the block area, ate an extra helping of snack, and even tried to use the toilet today. We are working on getting to the bathroom quickly enough. She did have an accident today, so there are clothes in her cubby that need washing. We will get there!"

Another example: "Good afternoon, Ms. Rajbhandari. How are you doing? I was wondering if you have a couple of extra minutes to talk about something that happened today with Ari. If not, it isn't urgent, but I would like to find time for us to talk without him present at some point in the next few days. I want to get your ideas and input."

Prearranged Meetings

Arranging a specific time and place to meet with a parent can work well for any communication, but it is necessary for sharing constructive information. Meeting separately allows for information to be shared privately and completely. Problems can be addressed, and successes can be shared. Conferences are one form of prearranged meeting that typically happen on a regular schedule each year. However, meetings with parents need not occur only on a regular schedule. They can happen whenever they're needed and can be initiated by either side.

No matter what time of day teachers and parents share information, they should remember positive communication strategies. These strategies support continued positive relationships and family engagement.

CHAPTER 4:
COMMUNICATION METHODS

Mr. Barundi dreads picking up his son, Arun, from his child care program. Arun has been biting other children. Every day brings a new biting incident and a new incident form to sign, acknowledging that his child is "that child." Arun's teacher, Ms. Claire, is sympathetic and tries to reassure Mr. Barundi that biting is developmentally appropriate for children Arun's age. Mr. Barundi is still worried that Arun will be asked to leave the child care program if he does not stop biting. He does not bite at home, but he is an only child and does not interact with other children his age at home. What more can Mr. Barundi and his wife do to help Arun stop biting? When does the biting go from developmentally appropriate to a severe problem? Perhaps Ms. Claire can offer some ideas if it happens again.

Verbal Communication

Sharing information verbally with parents, face to face, is the most common method of communicating about a child's day. When you are communicating verbally, it can be easy to share positive information but challenging to share constructive communication. No matter what you are sharing, use the utmost respect and care. This includes maintaining confidentiality. Never divulge the names of other involved children in conversation, even when parents prod you to do so. Confidentiality protects all parties from bias and retaliation. Additionally emotions run high when there are challenges in an early childhood program. When emotions run high, it can be easy to try to soothe feelings and soften reactions by providing more information than is advisable. It's critical that you maintain a calm and professional demeanor to set the tone and establish boundaries. Before you have a face-to-face discussion, organize your thoughts and the information you need to communicate. This strategy can help you communicate more effectively and ethically.

Three Pluses and a Wish

In this strategy, educators share three positive observations of the day and one aspect they wish the child to continue working on. This strategy provides parents with positive feedback on their child. It then offers an observation of a skill or a behavior that the educator believes needs improvement. This strategy sets a hopeful tone for the parent by stating multiple positive observations first, with a single constructive comment last. With the constructive comment at the end, the need for improvement is not lost within the positive comments.

Here's one example: "I want to share with you how friendly Jonas was today when his friend got hurt and was sad. Jonas brought his friend an ice pack and sat with him to read a book. Afterward they spent the afternoon creating in the sandbox together! We are still working with Jonas on being compassionate when other children want to play with him in the block area though. Today he was determined not to let others build with him, and he used his voice and hands to prevent them from playing there. We are helping him use a quieter voice and giving him words to express himself more gently."

Another example: "Today Tanesha spent much of the day sleeping in her crib, but when she was awake, she took all her bottles easily, and she lay on her back observing the mobile reflecting light from outside. It was quite beautiful! We are working on her tummy time, and she is not too happy about it! We will be easing her into it by just a few minutes each day, increasing about one minute per day until we are at, say, ten minutes of tummy time. We will be right by her during that time, encouraging her and offering her materials to catch her interest. She will get there!"

The Sandwich

Shifting verbal communication strategies can help educators shine a light where it is needed. The sandwich strategy is the one educators use most often when communicating information to a parent. Using this strategy, a teacher communicates a positive observation, then a concern or constructive feedback, and then finally, another positive observation. The advantage of the sandwich strategy is ending on a high note. However, when using this strategy, educators may forget the third part of the sandwich, omitting part of their message and ending on a low note. Additionally although it provides opportunities for multiple positive messages, those might overshadow the constructive message in the middle.

Here's one example: "I want to share with you that today Jonas helped his hurt friend feel better by offering him an ice pack and a book to read. We would like to see him this compassionate when he is playing in the block area and others want to join him. He uses a loud voice and his hands to let others know he does not want to play with them, and other children become mad. Jonas did, however, play with his friend in the sandbox all afternoon today."

Another example: "Tanesha spent much of the day sleeping and taking her bottles well. We are working on tummy time and lengthening it by one minute at a time. We are there with her, encouraging her to enjoy the time. She did enjoy lying on her back and watching the mobile hanging over her, reflecting the sun."

Technological Communication

Think of communication via technology as an extension of verbal communication. Some parents may actually prefer technological communication due to its ease and immediacy. Since parents cannot be with their children during the day, the use of technological communication increases opportunities to share daily happenings and draw parents in, increasing their engagement and support of the program. Communication technologies expand chances to share developmental progress, interests, challenges, and curriculum happenings with parents. Educators should be aware, however, that sensitive or constructive information shared with parents in writing can be misunderstood. No matter how parents prefer communication, teachers must ensure it is respectful and is received as intended.

Texting

Texting gives parents a chance to connect quickly and easily with their child's caregiver. For family child care programs, texting may be a quick way to ask and answer questions and distribute information. For center-based providers, texting families may not be allowed. Texting can take time away from caring for the children and may distract from safe practices. Additionally texting may tempt educators and parents to cross the line between professional and personal. Texting between programs and parents should be limited to immediate communication needs. It should be used only during time away from the children. If a program does not allow it, it should not be used.

If you use texting in your program, consider the following practices to maintain professionalism:

- Share only positive information.

- Use complete words and sentence structure, not text language.

- Reply or send only when you are not with the children.

Remind parents that your priority is to care for their children. You will reply to texts at your earliest convenience when you are away from the children.

Phone

The telephone is a tried-and-true communication method. Phone calls to or from parents provide real-time verbal communication from a distance. Phone calls should be conducted with the same care as in-person conversations. Communicating by phone also requires the following important considerations:

- Use your name and your program's name to introduce yourself.

- Tell parents immediately whether there is an emergency. Help ease their fears.

- Be aware of your tone. Remember to smile while you're speaking. Even though parents cannot see you smiling, they can hear it in your tone.

- Share positive information, no matter why you are calling.

- Use similar strategies as you would for face-to-face verbal communication.

- Remember that parents are at work, so keep your call brief. Arrange a specific meeting time if needed.

- Thank parents for their time and tell them you will see them later or the next day.

Here's one example: "Hello, Mr. Henning. This is Ms. Keesha from ABC Child Care Center, and I am calling to let you know some great news about your daughter Emma. There is no emergency, just a quick story to share about her day."

Another example: "Hello, Ms. Chen. This is Mr. Steve from ABC Child Care Center, and I am calling to talk with you briefly about an incident with Tin today. It is not an emergency, but I am hoping for a bit of your time. Are you available to speak for a few minutes, or can I call you back at a better time?"

When you receive phone calls from parents, follow these guidelines:

- Use a standard program greeting with a hello and your name.

- Ask how you can help.

- Listen before talking. Take a deep breath and count to three before responding.

- Take notes on the conversation.

- Use similar strategies as you would use for a face-to-face conversation.

- Be aware of your tone. Remember to smile; parents will hear it in your voice.

- Thank the parents for calling and tell them you will see them later or the next day.

Here's an example: "Hello. Thank you for calling ABC Child Care Center. This is Ms. Lu. How can I help you?"

Email

With email, educators and parents can ask and answer questions asynchronously. Both parties can respond when they're able. This means email is best for sharing information that does not need an immediate reply. It is a good means for sharing larger amounts of information or attachments. Take special care in composing email communications, as they are written documentation and can be easily stored and referred back to in the future. Make sure your emails are professional and communicate your intended messages.

When you are communicating through email, follow these guidelines:

- Use traditional professional greetings and signatures, such as *Hello, [name]*; *Dear [name]*; *thank you*; and *regards*.

- Write in complete sentences and use correct grammar, spelling, and punctuation.

- Be thorough but concise.

- Keep it simple. Provide information on only one item or issue in one email.

- Offer additional support or reading on the subject with an attachment or Internet link.

- Be aware of your tone and how you deliver information. Remember to think about your intentions and how your words could be received by parents.

- Do not expect responses immediately.

- Respond to emails within twenty-four hours of receipt and offer dates for providing any follow-ups.

Interactive Daily Communication Apps

Internet applications that offer communication via app text, chat, photos, videos, and attachments offer a unique and confidential means of communicating with families. With these apps, programs can take photos of the children in daily tasks and send them securely through the app to a parent or family member. For infants and toddlers, programs can track daily caregiving though the app, which automatically sends the information directly to the parents. When a program uses an app, there are no more stacks of daily sheets to track meals and diaper changes. All the information is in the app. Parents can also send observations and photos from their end to the program, which helps a picture of the whole child emerge. While apps can definitely offer advantages to programs and parents, they are costly, require wireless Internet, and often require the use of a tablet or smartphone for taking photos and composing documentation. The cost can be prohibitive. Nevertheless such apps are quickly becoming the new normal.

Newsletters

Newsletters are another useful form of communication between programs and families. Newsletters can be printed on paper, sent via email, or posted on websites. No matter how the newsletter is distributed, it can offer a large amount of information to families, helping them stay informed and inviting them to be engaged in their child's program. Here are ten tips for creating engaging and helpful newsletters for families:

- Send the newsletter on a regular and predictable schedule.

- Keep a consistent format with each issue.

- Provide updates from each program or for each age group.

- Provide curriculum highlights for developmental domains.

- Share program-wide events and reminders.

- Share information on a hot topic for parents.

- Take a poll or ask survey questions and request a response.

- Provide policy reminders and highlights.

- Provide a calendar of upcoming important dates occurring before the next newsletter.

- Use your program logo and name prominently.

CHAPTER 5: SHARING CHILDREN'S LEARNING

Ms. Peterson loves when her daughter, Kirsten, comes home from child care with artwork. She enjoys posting the art on her bulletin board at work. The tiny handprints and colorful pictures help her stay positive during her long workdays. She knows her daughter is happy at child care. But even though Kirsten is only three years old, Ms. Peterson worries that her daughter will not be ready for kindergarten. At pickup time, Kirsten is often playing in the kitchen area with other children. Kirsten's teacher tells her how much Kirsten enjoys painting, digging in the sensory table, and playing house in the dramatic play area. Ms. Peterson does not know if Kirsten can recognize shapes, letters, and numbers or how her writing compares to her peers'. When will Kirsten start learning how to read? How will painting and playing house help her be prepared for kindergarten? Ms. Peterson wishes she knew more about what her daughter is learning each day.

Documentation of Learning

To help families understand your curriculum and how their children are learning and growing in your program, display examples and descriptions of children's work. Many programs do post examples of children's work, but they may not include any information on what it took for the children to create the work. Showing families the process helps them see the learning objectives and the experience as well. Following are some tips for displaying documentation of children's learning for families:

- Post work by all children or develop a rotating system.

- Label the front of the work with the child's first name.

- Take photos of the creation process.

- Write or type out the steps of the creative process.

- Write or type out the learning objectives or competencies accomplished in the process.

- Display the creative process and objectives alongside the examples and photos.

Conferences and Meetings

For most early childhood programs, parent-teacher conferences are a normal part of the yearly calendar. Meeting with families to share their children's learning and growth is a chance to build stronger relationships and engagement. The key to successful parent-teacher conferences is remembering that a conference is a conversation between parent and teacher, not a report to the parents about the child. The conversation is meant to be about the child's individual development and growth, along with a plan for helping the child continue on that path. If concerns arise with a child's development, conferences are a chance to discuss the situation in detail and establish plans for supporting the child through the challenge. Conferences offer an opportunity to work as a team to support the needs of the child and the family.

Timing

Conferences can happen at any time, not just at scheduled times. Conferences should happen throughout the year to share progress in growth and development. At the very least, conferences should happen at the following times in an early childhood program:

- **With enrollment:** This conference is the intake meeting with the family, at which the educators and the family are getting to know one another.

- **At least annually, and preferably every six months:** Conferences should occur on a regular schedule during the child's enrollment—at least annually, and preferably every six months. This allows for regular communication and discussion of progress. It also allows both sides to share more information and continue to develop the picture of the whole child.

- **With a transition to the next age group:** Conferences prior to a child's transition to the next age group provide a chance to share developmental progress and encourage questions about new expectations. For center-based programs, this is a perfect time to provide a handoff from one educator to the next.

- **Before leaving the program:** When a child is ready to leave a program, due to aging out or for other reasons, a meeting with the family to discuss their child's growth and experience is helpful for both the program and the family. The family gets a chance to be updated on their child's strengths and areas to grow, while the educators learn about their program through the family's eyes.

- **At the family's request:** Conferences and meetings must always occur when families request them. Parents think about their child constantly, and they only want what is best for their children. They are their children's primary caregivers and first teachers. When parents ask for a conference or a meeting, it is always because they are placing their child first and want more information so they can continue to do so.

What Conferences Are and Aren't

A conference is all of these things:

- a meeting of the minds about a child's well-being

- a sharing of information

- an opportunity for setting goals based upon common knowledge

- a formal opportunity to share developmental progress

- a give-and-take of information, observations, and stories about a child

- a positive back-and-forth conversation

- a chance to problem solve together when challenges arise

- an opportunity to give families supportive parenting resources

A conference is not any of these things:

- an opportunity to share only constructive information

- a chance to present a comprehensive dossier on the child's development and behavior

- a time for only the educator to talk

- a time to talk about other children in the program

- a chance to compare a child to siblings or other children

- a time to gossip

Conferences should include the following elements:

- developmental domain progress based on agreed-upon learning standards (perhaps a published assessment system or state-specific learning standards)

- examples of a child's work and developmental progress based on age level

- photos and videos of the child in action during regularly scheduled activities

- previous developmental assessments

- open-ended questions for the parents about their observations on the child's developmental progress

- goal setting in conjunction with the parents

- time to talk openly and without rushing

- paper and writing utensils to record notes, observations, stories, and goals

Challenges with Conferences

Conference time can be one of the most challenging times of the year for educators. The following paragraphs describe several common challenges.

Parents Who Do Not Attend

A key concern educators mention is that parents do not have the time or interest to attend conferences. In truth parents often just do not know what to expect. When they think of conferences, they imagine only a chance to talk about their child negatively. To combat this perception, be sure to discuss the positive aspects of conferences in the first meeting with a family. Explain how a conference is an opportunity for families to share their children's experiences, development, and stories so that the program can learn more about their children.

Additionally offer conferences over a longer period of time, or space them out throughout the year. Open scheduling allows for less stress and more flexibility. You could also host conferences via a web meeting tool or through a video chat. Video conferencing prevents the need to travel, allowing parents to join from their home or workplace.

Delivering Sensitive or Constructive Information

It is never easy to share sensitive or constructive information with parents. Parents want to see their child as perfect. Nevertheless it is our responsibility as educators to give parents honest and helpful information about their child's development. When you are delivering constructive information, be sensitive to the fact that parents may not want to hear it. Provide examples and avoid judgment. Refrain from offering your opinion, and instead stick to the observable facts. Avoid using words such as *challenging*, *frustrated*, or *abnormal*. Use communication strategies, such as those described in chapter 4, to provide positive and constructive information.

When you are delivering sensitive and constructive information, be sure to also include solutions you can try in your program. How will the program support this child's situation? What is already being done (or what has been done) to support the child, and how did it work out? Be ready to share what progress is already happening and what additional tools are available.

Parents Who Are Opposed to Program Policy or Curriculum Goals

Programs must remember that not all parents are a good fit for their program, and not all children will thrive in all programs. At the same time, providing early childhood education and care for young children is a service business. Caregivers and educators serve the children enrolled and their parents. Providing a service to families means working as hard as possible to help them be satisfied and to help their children do their very best.

When parents do not agree with the program philosophy or curriculum, it is important to listen carefully to their views. It may well be that their philosophy and expectations for their child do not match those of the program. It may also be that the family does not understand the philosophy or has been receiving conflicting information. Listen carefully to the parents' concerns and ask questions. Seek to understand. It is possible that a family may not want to stay with the program, but this situation may offer a chance to learn more from one another.

Delivering Information about Developmental Concerns

Parents count on early childhood educators to be experts in child development, regardless of whether we feel like experts. When our observation raises red flags about a child's development, we have a duty to share that observation with the child's parents.

When you need to share developmental concerns, you must do so only in a one-on-one conference with the family. Remember that since parents are a child's first and most important teachers, they want to see their child as perfect. Your sensitivity in explaining your concerns is crucial. It affects not only parents' ability to see you as professional and caring, but also parents' reactions to what they hear. Deliver information in terms of your observations—describe what you have seen and heard. Educators are not doctors, so refrain from making a diagnosis or sharing your opinion. Instead ask questions to gain more information, and share resources with parents. Assure parents that you will provide the support they need to seek additional help. They may take it hard. They may not. Nevertheless you have shared your concerns based on your factual observations and your educational knowledge.

If you work in a center-based program, be sure to share your concerns with the program director before discussing them with the family. Work together to identify resources to share and to determine what the program can do to help.

CHAPTER 6: PARTICIPATION AND ENGAGEMENT

Min and her little brother, Daniel, have been attending the program since Min turned three. Min is now ready to move on to kindergarten, and her brother is almost three. He will be moving to the preschool room in the fall. Min's parents have wanted to participate in activities at the program for some time, but with their work schedules, they often arrive late or have to miss them altogether. Additionally Min and Daniel do not celebrate the same holidays most children in the program seem to celebrate. Most of the family engagement activities at the program are based on these common holidays, such as Halloween and Christmas. Min and Daniel's parents would love to be more involved for their children's sake, but they just do not see the opportunity, even if they had the time.

For many programs, family engagement opportunities begin and end with program-wide events and activities. But for many parents, engagement needs to be entirely different. They already have a full calendar of family and work responsibilities; adding program events or activities may be impossible. How, then, can programs involve all families better and meet all children's needs? Programs must see engagement as any and all participation and interest in supporting the program.

Meet Families Where They Are

Provide opportunities for families to participate from wherever they are, in whatever ways they can. If your program offers a variety of options, such as those in the following list, parents will be better able to participate. They can choose activities based on their ability at the time.

- **In-person engagement:** opportunities for parents to be physically present in the program with their child, such as curriculum nights, lunch and learns, conferences, guest reading times, or program events

- **Virtual engagement:** opportunities to join conversations or events from a distance, such as virtual meetings, webinars, conferences by video chat, parent group meetings, and virtual guest readers

- **In-kind engagement:** donations of food, materials, and toys, such as for food drives and clothing drives, or time, such as building a climber, gardening, recording books on tape, addressing envelopes, or maintaining the program website

Embed Engagement Opportunities in the Learning Environment

A family-centered approach means that the program welcomes all families and encourages them to be involved with all aspects of the program. It means that the program considers families' interests in every aspect of the program. Encouraging family engagement in every aspect of the program is a challenge, but it is necessary for building a culture of family engagement.

Guests

Here are just a few of the ways in which guests—parents and other adult family members—can be involved in daily program activities:

- **Guest readers:** A guest reader reads a book or two with a group of children during a group time or story time. Vary story times by hosting a surprise guest reader (the guest is a total surprise to the children), a bilingual guest reader (the guest reads books in a home language and in English), or even a video guest reader (the guest reads aloud via video chat).

- **Guest musicians:** Guest musicians are similar to guest readers, but they share their musical talents instead. Guests might play an instrument or sing—or both—depending on their personal talent.

- **Guest artists:** Guest artists can come to the program to share their artistic talents, from painting and sculpting to acting and dancing.

- **Guest chefs:** A guest chef shares a cooking project with the children. This guest is most appropriate with preschoolers and older children. Guest chefs offer a great way for families to share valued family recipes and cultural traditions with friends in the program.

Meals and Snacks

Around the world, people value meals as times to gather together and learn about one another. Likewise meals in early childhood education are a time to talk about the day and about children's interests. Inviting families to join their children for meals and snacks is a way to bring children and families together. Here are a few ways to do that:

- **Snack with a guest day:** Invite a parent or another family member to a snacktime once per month. Set the table for an afternoon snack together. Vary this activity with an occasional surprise guest.

- **Picnic meal or snack:** Invite family members to attend a picnic meal or snack in the spring or summer. Sit outside and enjoy time together as a group. Invite the guests to stay for the next activity.

- **Winter picnic dinner:** Plan an after-hours dinner picnic, with families bringing their preferred picnic main dish, sides, and blanket. The program provides healthy drinks and a healthy dessert made by the children during the day. Hold the picnic inside in the winter, with blankets on the program floor.

- **Program progressive dinner:** This progressive dinner has parents providing potluck items based upon their child's age group. For example, in a center-based program, infant families can bring appetizers, toddler families can bring side dishes, and preschooler families can bring main dishes. The program can provide healthy drinks and dessert. As the dinner continues, parents and children move from one room to the next, visiting and meeting parents and children from all age groups. Family child care programs can host a similar event by dividing the meal among the age groups or evenly among families and serving the various dishes in different places around the program.

Everyday Activities

The everyday activities children experience are often the least shared by programs that are seeking family interest and engagement. Too often programs invite family members only to the special events, such as a visit by a firefighter or a dentist. Opportunities like these are fun, but they aren't the only possibilities. Consider inviting family members and encouraging involvement in everyday activities, too. Where in your program can parents and family members join in? Consider the following:

- **Outside play:** In the outdoor environment, parents can join in with gardening, building snow sculptures, digging in the sand, or baking in a mud kitchen.

- **Group time:** During group time, parents can offer additional laps for sitting, a change in reader, or expertise in music or dance.

- **Writing center:** Parents can take dictation for children's story writing, or they can help children create books.

- **Art center:** Parents are naturally creative in an early childhood art center. Invite those with design interests or artistic talents to work with the children on opening up their imaginations.

Special Events and Experiences

Special events and experiences happen frequently in programs. Events may specifically include parents and families, or they may be designed especially for the children. Regardless these events and activities must reflect the culture of family engagement you wish to see in your program.

Holidays and Birthdays

Holiday celebrations are common in early childhood programs. Programs may honor mainstream secular American holidays, such as Halloween or Saint Patrick's Day, or they may celebrate more religious holidays, such as Christmas or Easter. It's important to remember that not all families celebrate all holidays. Depending on your program, including all families in holiday celebrations may be difficult. Being aware of the religious and cultural preferences of your program's families will help you choose holidays or celebrations that best reflect your families.

Celebrating birthdays can also raise questions. Religious practices may influence if and how families celebrate birthdays. Be aware of family preferences before celebrating birthdays so you do not inadvertently offend a family.

Which Holidays Should Programs Celebrate?

A program's best bet is to honor the holidays that its families honor. But what about families who believe that holidays are best celebrated at home? What if one family does not celebrate any holidays? How does a program truly honor all families?

Instead of celebrating holidays, programs can encourage families to celebrate their own cherished holidays first with their children. After the holiday has ended, the program can offer the children a chance to share what they did with their family or share activities with the other children. Here's an example: Children first celebrate Thanksgiving with their families. Upon returning from the holiday break, the program can ask what the children were thankful for and how they celebrated the holiday with their families. Those who do not celebrate Thanksgiving can share about how they spent their long weekend and what they are thankful for in their life.

What about Nonreligious Holidays Such as Mother's Day or Father's Day?

Consider a child who is living with a foster family or a child whose mother died in childbirth. What about children who have never known their fathers or children being raised by grandparents? So many children live in family configurations that are not represented by traditional Mother's Day and Father's Day celebrations. Such celebrations can lead to misunderstandings and sadness for the children. Asking a motherlike or fatherlike figure to step in may help in the short term, but it does not help the program develop an inclusive family culture.

An alternative is to simply let families honor Mother's Day and Father's Day on their own, in their own way. Between the two holidays, a program can offer a Family Day to celebrate all members of the child's family.

Here's an example: On Family Day, children invite members of their family to come to the program, or they make gifts and cards and share stories about the family members they hold dear. Instead of singling out just mothers and fathers, Family Day supports children from all kinds of families, such as those led by LGBTQ parents, single parents, grandparents, aunts and uncles, foster parents, and even older siblings.

How Do We Decide What Holidays to Celebrate?

Use the intake meeting and parent-teacher conferences to discover your families' cultural and religious traditions and preferences. Take a moment to ask them how they prefer to celebrate holidays with their children. Consider, then, how you can incorporate their preferences into the program.

CHAPTER 7: INVESTING IN FAMILIES WITH A RESOURCE LIBRARY

As a single parent, Portia always feels ten steps behind. Her children, Erik and Marta, deserve for her to be a better parent, but she only has so much time in a day. Because Portia is working full time while going to school, Erik and Marta have a full day at child care and then spend the evening with Grandma. During the week, Portia often sees her children only when she tucks them into bed at night. She heard that reading with children helps them learn to read; at least Grandma helps with that. On weekends Portia enjoys spending time with her children, but she does not always know what to do or where to go. Money is an issue, and everything worthwhile is expensive. Eventually Portia will be able to provide more for her children.

Developing a culture of family engagement takes time. Relationship building takes time. There is no magic spell to make everyone get along or to make every parent engage deeply in your program. Instead celebrate every positive situation, word, collaboration, and interaction. Realize that every effort makes a difference and that every effort builds upon the one before it, making the fabric of the relationship stronger. Never give up. If a curriculum event has only one family attend, it is a success! Make sure to offer it again, show pictures, and share the positive effects. More families will come the next time. Remember that building a culture of family engagement is an everyday effort. Consider creating a library of resources to support that effort. These resources may be for your program staff, families, or both. In any case, it will be much easier to share resources when you already have them at your fingertips.

Building Resources and References

Your library of resources to support children and families should be immense! In this day and age, with the wide availability of digital materials that can be easily emailed or posted online, we are rich in resources for parenting support. Of course some resources can do more harm than good, so it is up to early childhood educators to identify credible, supportive, and helpful resources for the families in our programs.

When you are providing resources to families, consider the following issues:

Credibility

- Ensure that any article, pamphlet, or website you recommend is research based.

- Websites ending in *.org*, *.edu*, or *.gov* often provide the most credible information. The following websites are a few good examples:

  American Academy of Pediatrics (www.aap.org)

  Pacer Center (www.pacer.org)

  Parents as Teachers (parentsasteachers.org)

  National Association for the Education of Young Children (www.naeyc.org)

  Zero to Three (www.zerotothree.org)

  Child Care Aware (www.childcareaware.org)

  Center for Parent Information and Resources (www.parentcenterhub.org)

  National Association for Family Child Care (www.nafcc.org)

  Parent to Parent USA (www.p2pusa.org)

- Before recommending a blog, make sure the writer has an early childhood education background. Research the writer to rule out the possibility of an agenda that is not based on research evidence.

- Check that resources are current and published within the past few years. Research on child development is happening constantly, and the most recent information will be the most supportive to children and families.

- It is fine to have some tried-and-true resources in your library as well. For example, resources written by noted theorists or psychologists, such as David Elkind, T. Berry Brazelton, and Mary Sheedy Kurcinka, will stand the test of time.

Developmentally Appropriate Practice (DAP)

- Read through each resource to make sure it supports developmentally appropriate practice (DAP) (Copple and Bredekamp 2009) with families and children.

- Distribute only what is age appropriate and individually appropriate for children and families. Sometimes information should go to just one family, and sometimes it is appropriate for a whole group of families.

Program Support

- Be sure your program is willing to support the advice being shared with families, such as if a resource discusses possible challenges to your guidance policy.

- Share all materials with program staff. Keep everyone up on the latest, most relevant research.

Creating Your Own Parent and Family Resources

Providing a space within your program to offer parents and families helpful information can go far in supporting family needs each and every day. This space can be both a physical space and an online presence. Customize your space to meet your program's and families' needs. Get creative and use this space to share your expertise. Consider including the following types of resources:

Periodicals

Provide copies of professional early childhood periodicals focusing on child development and early childhood education. Recommended publications include the following:

- *Young Children*
- *Exchange*
- *Early Childhood Today*
- *Parents*

Resource Books

Provide copies of professional resource books offering support on everything from child development to guidance and discipline, nutrition, health and safety, and more. In your library, reflect the subjects the parents and families in your program need the most. Parents can check out books for their own growth and development as well as their children's.

Articles and Brochures

Collect articles and brochures gathered through everyday practice on topics of interest and need for families. Create binders or electronic files on a shared website for quick reference. Add or replace resources on a regular basis to keep articles current and on topics of the most interest to your families. In a regular newsletter, let parents know what is currently available.

Newsletter Library

If your program provides regular newsletters for families, be sure to keep them in a binder available for parents to review at their leisure. The binder can also be a quick reference guide to policies and procedures.

Policies and Procedures Handbook

Keep a copy of your program's policies and procedures handbook available for family and staff reference. This can be a physical copy, in the lobby or near the entrance of the program, and also digital, on your program's website.

Visual Documentation of Learning

Offer photos and descriptions of children participating in everyday tasks, activities, and special events. Provide information on the early learning standards exhibited and how children are learning and growing through each activity. Rotate displays between age groups and types of activities to keep them current and to boost interest.

Take-Home Literacy Kits

A love of reading is cultivated by parents and children reading together. For some families, high-quality children's books are not accessible. Create literacy kits, each containing a children's book and storytelling props or writing materials, that families can check out for a few days to use at home. Children might want to bring back photos of reading with their families. You can post these for all to see.

Monthly Guidance Tips

Guidance practices are a hot topic for parents and educators alike, as they work with children through behavior challenges. Provide a monthly tip for parents highlighting a best practice, such as for redirection, problem solving, or aggression. Teach parents strategies now—before they even know they need them—so they'll have them in hand later, when needed.

Curriculum Highlights

Highlighting special events in the program can offer families confirmation that the program goes above and beyond for their children's education. These curriculum highlights can include posting photos, examples of work, and child and parent descriptions of events. These program-wide events can also bring the program community closer together.

Community Events

Families are often looking for interesting and inexpensive community events or activities to participate in with their children. Use your resource space for providing information about the local community's recreation programs, parks, and libraries; free events at local businesses; and other special seasonal activities. Partner with local agencies and businesses to promote family-friendly activities and events.

CHAPTER 8: ADVOCATING FOR THE BEST FOR CHILDREN AND FAMILIES

Ms. Galinda has worked with infants and their families for almost twenty years. She has seen firsthand how high-quality child care positively influences children's development and supports families. While she was completing her bachelor's degree, Ms. Galinda learned that the first five years of life, when the brain is growing at its fastest rate, are the most important years in a child's development. Capitalizing on this time in life provides children with the strongest foundation for success in both school and life. After hearing recent news reports concerning the high cost of good-quality child care, Ms. Galinda has decided it is time to share her knowledge and stand up for the accessibility of high-quality child care. Now she is wondering where she should start.

To advocate for children and families means to stand up for and promote best practices, which improve systems and children's outcomes. Often people perceive advocacy only as protesting legislation with marches and picket signs, but advocacy for children and families is much more than that. It includes sharing information and professional perspectives on early childhood education and care issues with stakeholders. Stakeholders may include the following:

- community leaders

- local government officials

- early childhood education colleagues

- state government legislators and officials

- federal government legislators and officials

- organizational leaders

- business leaders

- parents

- community members

Some stakeholders, such as legislators, can create and vote on state standards affecting quality child care or on how much the state will subsidize child care costs for families. Other stakeholders can simply spread the good news about your program and how it prepares children for public school. Regardless of who your stakeholders are, sharing information and perspectives with them can boost family engagement by building awareness of issues important to your families.

What to Share with Stakeholders

So what should programs be prepared to share with stakeholders? Share your expertise with early childhood education and care, and your passion for doing what is best for children. Your expertise may teach a stakeholder about language development, how children learn social skills through play, or how high-quality programs support the whole family. Your expertise may make a difference in how family issues are perceived in the community and set a precedent for future early childhood education policy. Here are some topics on which you might share your expertise:

- best practices for growth and development

- best practices for health, safety, and nutrition

- curriculum activities that promote school readiness

- the impact of child care quality on parents and families

- the impact of the cost of care on families

Communicating Your Message

How can programs share information and perspectives with stakeholders? There is no single best way to communicate your messages about children, families, education, and care. Get creative and share your energy in whatever way feels comfortable. Legislators will often say that it was one particular story from one family that swayed their perspective on a particular issue involving children and families. It does not take a big event to make a big impact. Think "small but mighty"! Here are some ways you might communicate with stakeholders:

- Invite stakeholders to your program to see the program in action and meet families.

- Write regularly to stakeholders via email and snail mail, sharing information and even examples of children's work.

- Encourage parents and family members to share their child care stories in their home communities.

- Attend community events and activities on behalf of your program to spread the good news of the program's culture of family engagement.

Through your advocacy, your families will know that you are on their side and that you want to invest in their future. It might just be your story, or that of a family in your program, that will make a difference in policy or practice for all families.

APPENDIX A: FAMILY VISIT RECORD

Please provide the information below to help us get to know you.

Family Name	Parent or Guardian First Name	Child(ren)'s First Name	Age of Child(ren)	Phone	Email

APPENDIX B: INTAKE INTERVIEW QUESTIONS

When you are developing your program's intake questionnaire, tailor it to meet the child's age and development. Some questions are for specific age groups, and others are for all ages. In your effort to build a culture of family engagement, you can ask the following questions of families who have children of all ages.

1. Tell me about your family. Who lives in the family home? What is the language spoken most at home?

2. What are your most precious family traditions?

3. What are your family's practices around food or mealtimes? Do you usually eat family meals or eat on the run? Do you have any special dietary preferences or needs? What are your child(ren)'s favorite foods?

4. Tell me about your hopes for your child.

5. Tell me your expectations for your child.

6. Tell me about any fears you have for your child.

7. Do you have any nondevelopmental concerns about or for your child?

8. What would you like to see in your child's program?

9. Do you have any concerns or questions about your child's development? Does your child have any identified special needs?

10. Has your child traveled to locations outside our community? With family or to see family? Identify locations and length of time away.

11. Tell me about your child's typical day at home. What is your child's morning routine, schedule, evening routine, and bedtime?

12. What is your child's favorite activity to play alone?

13. What is your child's favorite activity to play with others (siblings, peers, neighbors, adults)?

14. Does your child have any specific fears?

15. Did your child attend another program previously? Tell me about your child's typical day at that program.

16. How do you prefer to receive information about your child's activities and experiences at our program?

17. What do you want to know most about your child's day?

18. Our program values your involvement. How would you like to be involved or engaged in the program? Do you have any concerns or limitations regarding family engagement, such as work commitments or transportation needs?

19. What are some skills, interests, talents, or hobbies that you might share with our program?

20. What are your feelings and preferences surrounding holidays, special dates, and birthdays? Are there any special holidays that your family celebrates or does not celebrate? Do you have any concerns about celebrations in general?

21. What special family activities or events do you do throughout the year (weekly, monthly, annually, around holidays, and so on)?

22. Parenting is a tough job. What additional information or support might you need or want to support you in this job?

APPENDIX C: NEWSLETTER TEMPLATE

| **Program Name and Logo** |
| **Month and Year** |

Note or update from director or owner:

This section should be a personal note sharing thoughts and inspiration for the upcoming time period. It can be brief or more in depth. You can use photos (with family permission) or clip art to make this section pop. This is your space to share information about yourself, as well as your hopes and dreams for the program and the children.

Calendar list of upcoming events or save the dates:

This section is for a list of important dates for families to remember, such as conferences, curriculum nights, special guest days, and field trips.

Policy or program reminders or details about an upcoming program-wide event or activity:

This section is for details surrounding an upcoming or past event, specific policy updates, reminders or changes, curriculum highlights, or other exciting program announcements.

Program highlights (Example: What's going on with our infants and toddlers?):

This section should be brief, highlighting happenings in the program for a specific age group, classroom, or designated group of children. It can include photos, descriptions, examples of work, and even quotes by the children, if applicable. Ultimately it should encourage parents and families to visit the program for more information, such as by directing them to a documentation display or examples of work.

Program highlights (Example: What's going on with our preschoolers?):

This section should be brief, highlighting happenings in the program for a specific age group, classroom, or designated group of children. It can include photos, descriptions, examples of work, and even quotes by the children, if applicable. Ultimately it should encourage parents and families to visit the program for more information, such as by directing them to a documentation display or examples of work.

Program Name and Logo **Month and Year** (*continued*)	

Program highlights (Example: What's going on with our _____?): This section should be brief, highlighting happenings in the program for a specific age group, classroom, or designated group of children. It can include photos, descriptions, examples of work, and even quotes by the children, if applicable. Ultimately it should encourage parents and families to visit the program for more information, such as by directing them to a documentation display or examples of work.	**Photo highlighting a special activity or a beloved daily event at the program**

Parent education or support:

In this section, include some helpful information and support on a particular topic of interest for the parents in your program. This topic can be targeted to a specific age group (such as biting) or can be universal (such as picky eaters). Offer tips and strategies in a bulleted, quick-reference format. Use and provide credible resources and references. Additional links for follow-up are also helpful.

Educator spotlight: In this section, highlight an educator in your program. Share information such as education, experience with children, favorite parts of the day, and special interests. Educators can write this information themselves. This section can also include information about an educator's family and a photo. Professionalism is a priority.	**Contact information and communication reminders:** In this section, provide your program's contact information and preferences. Include names, phone numbers, email addresses, program hours, and other useful details.

APPENDIX D: CONFERENCE QUESTIONS

No matter which observation and assessment measure your program employs, asking the right questions and sharing the right information at a conference will greatly improve family engagement and put the picture of the whole child into focus.

Questions to Ask

1. Tell me how your child is doing at home. What are your observations? How do you think your child is doing at the program?

2. What are the strengths you see in your child?

3. What are the areas for growth you see in your child?

4. Do you have any concerns about your child's development at this age?

5. Do you have any worries about the future? Is there anything that makes you nervous about your child's development or growth?

6. What would you like to see your child do or accomplish while in this program?

7. What do you enjoy most about your child?

8. What is something you want me to know about your child?

9. What can I or the program do to better support your child?

10. What can I or the program do to better support you in your role as a parent?

Information to Share

- **Academic standards:** These might be state standards, accreditation standards, or program-specific standards. Whatever assessment tools your program uses to track developmental or academic progress, explain how they work and why they are important for this child.

- **Curriculum approach:** Explain your program's curriculum approach (such as Creative Curriculum, High-Scope, or project-based learning) and how it will benefit this child.

- **Curriculum ideas:** Instead of simply telling families what they can do with their child at home, provide ideas in materials they can take with them to do at home, such as song lyrics, cooking recipes, activity recipes, and community field trip ideas.

- **Developmental next steps:** Provide supportive information about the next steps in the child's development and what the family can expect in the different developmental domains. Keep it brief and easy to understand so families are not overwhelmed. Be sure to tailor the information to the individual children and families; that is, do not provide the exact same information for every child in the age group.

REFERENCES

Copple, Carol, and Sue Bredekamp, eds. 2009. *Developmentally Appropriate Practice in Early Childhood Programs.* Washington, DC: NAEYC.

Donohue, Chip. 2017. "Digital Age Family Engagement: The Role of Media Mentors." *Exchange* March/April, 12–14.

Heick, Terry. 2013. "Parents: 19 Meaningful Questions You Should Ask Your Child's Teacher." *Edutopia.* Accessed August 19, 2017. www.edutopia.org/blog/19-questions-for-parents -terry-heick.

Kenny, Erin Kathleen. 2014. "Goodness of Fit." *Exchange* November/December, 82–85.

Merriam-Webster. 2017. s.v. "Culture." Accessed August 18, 2017. www.merriam-webster.com /dictionary/culture.

NAEYC (National Association for the Education of Young Children). 2011. "NAEYC Code of Ethical Conduct and Statement of Commitment." *NAEYC.* www.naeyc.org/sites/default /files/globally-shared/downloads/PDFs/resources/position-statements/Ethics%20 Position%20Statement2011_09202013update.pdf.

Powell, Douglas R., and Patrick M. O'Leary. 2009. "Strengthening Relations between Parents and Early Childhood Programs." In *Informing Our Practice: Useful Research on Young Children's Development*, first edition, edited by Eva L. Essa and Melissa M. Burnham, 193–202. Washington, DC: NAEYC.

Walsh, Froma. 2004. "A Family Resilience Framework: Innovative Practice Applications." *Family Relations* 51, no. 2, 130–37. https://doi.org/10.1111/j.1741-3729.2002.00130.x.

Printed in the USA
CPSIA information can be obtained
at www.ICGtesting.com
JSHW062025301223
54535JS00008B/15